BRAVE THE BIOME
MOUNTAIN
[SURVIVAL GUIDE]

[CYNTHIA O'BRIEN]

CRABTREE
PUBLISHING COMPANY
WWW.CRABTREEBOOKS.COM

BRAVE THE BIOME

Author: Cynthia O'Brien

Editors: Sarah Eason, Jennifer Sanderson, and Ellen Rodger

Proofreader and indexer: Tracey Kelly

Proofreader: Petrice Custance

Editorial director: Kathy Middleton

Design: Jessica Moon

Cover design: Tammy McGarr

Photo research: Rachel Blount

Production coordinator and Prepress technician: Tammy McGarr

Print coordinator: Katherine Berti

Consultant: David Hawksett

Produced for Crabtree Publishing by Calcium

Photo Credits:
t=Top, c=Center, b=Bottom, l= Left, r=Right

Inside: Jessica Moon: p. 13b; Shutterstock: Alexander P: p. 19b; ArtMari: pp. 7t, 23b; BGSmith: pp. 24–25; Alex Brylov: pp. 6–7; CartoonDesignerFX: p. 16b; CGN089: pp. 26–27; Olga Danylenko: pp. 4–5, 32; EB Adventure Photography: pp. 28–29; Fineart1: p. 10t; Gestalt Imagery: pp. 8–9; Wlad Go: p. 18b; Yevgen Kravchenko: p. 29t; Blazej Lyjak: p. 23t; Lzf: p. 24t; James Aloysius Mahan V: p. 12t; Masbey: p. 10b; Vitalii Matokha: p. 15r; Christopher Meder: p. 9r; Mikolajn: pp. 30–31; My Good Images: pp. 18–19; OutdoorWorks: pp. 12–13; Duet PandG: p. 27l; PlusONE: p. 6b; Daniel Prudek: p. 5t; Scott E Read: p. 25b; Adam Reck: pp. 22–23; Joshua Resnick: p. 17b; Sirtravelalot: p. 22b; Bodor Tivadar: p. 25t; TSN52: pp. 16–17; Carlos Bruzos Valin: pp. 14–15; Vixit: pp. 20–21; Yanik88: pp. 10–11.

Cover: All images from Shutterstock

Library and Archives Canada Cataloguing in Publication

Title: Mountain survival guide / Cynthia O'Brien.
Names: O'Brien, Cynthia (Cynthia J.), author.
Description: Series statement: Brave the biome | Includes index.
Identifiers: Canadiana (print) 20200286064 |
  Canadiana (ebook) 20200286080 |
  ISBN 9780778781349 (softcover) |
  ISBN 9780778781288 (hardcover) |
  ISBN 9781427125743 (HTML)
Subjects: LCSH: Wilderness survival—Juvenile literature. |
  LCSH: Survival—Juvenile literature. |
  LCSH: Mountains—Juvenile literature.
Classification: LCC GV200.5 .O27 2021 | DDC j613.6/909143—dc23

Library of Congress Cataloging-in-Publication Data

Names: O'Brien, Cynthia, author.
Title: Mountain survival guide / Cynthia O'Brien.
Description: New York : Crabtree Publishing Company, [2021] |
  Series: Brave the biome | Includes index.
Identifiers: LCCN 2020029913 (print) | LCCN 2020029914 (ebook) |
  ISBN 9780778781288 (hardcover) |
  ISBN 9780778781349 (paperback) |
  ISBN 9781427125743 (ebook)
Subjects: LCSH: Mountaineering--Juvenile literature. |
  Survival--Juvenile literature.
Classification: LCC GV200 .O27 2021 (print) | LCC GV200 (ebook)
  | DDC 796.522--dc23
LC record available at https://lccn.loc.gov/2020029913
LC ebook record available at https://lccn.loc.gov/2020029914

Crabtree Publishing Company

www.crabtreebooks.com   1-800-387-7650

Printed in the U.S.A./092020/CG20200810

Published in Canada
Crabtree Publishing
616 Welland Ave.
St. Catharines, Ontario
L2M 5V6

Published in the United States
Crabtree Publishing
347 Fifth Ave.
Suite 1402-145
New York, NY 10016

Published in the United Kingdom
Crabtree Publishing
Maritime House
Basin Road North, Hove
BN41 1WR

Published in Australia
Crabtree Publishing
3 Charles Street
Coburg North
VIC, 3058

CONTENTS

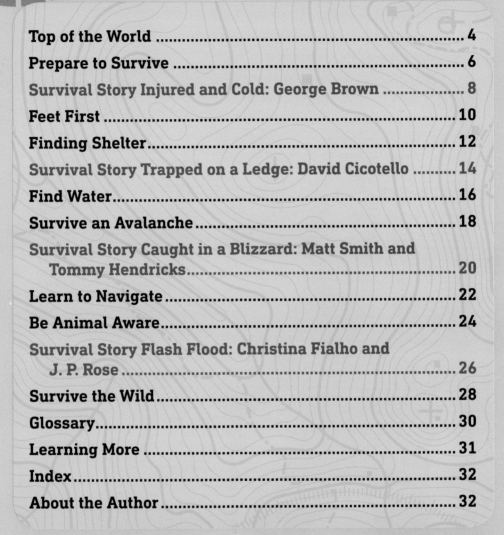

A mountain is a large landform that rises above the surrounding land. The world's highest peak, or mountaintop, is Mount Everest. It is in the Himalayan Mountain **Range** in Asia, and it rises 29,029 feet (8,848 m). The Rocky Mountains stretch from western British Columbia, Canada, to New Mexico in the United States. Other ranges include the Alps in Europe and the Andes in South America. Most mountains have peaks, but some have plateaus, which are surrounding areas of flat land.

THE MOUNTAIN BIOME

Mountain **biome** explorers must be prepared for different environments. The lower levels of mountains and valleys may be covered in trees or may be areas of desert or **tundra**. As mountains rise higher, the trees cannot grow. The place the trees stop growing is called the tree line. It will be rockier after the tree line, but **alpine** plants such as moss grow close to the ground. Many higher mountain ranges have **glaciers** and snow. Most of the world's rivers start as small streams in the mountains. They become larger as snow, rain, and other streams feed them as they flow down the mountain. Mountains supply more than half the world's fresh water.

In the mountains, there may be no help nearby. Watching for natural resources, such as water, and being able to use them safely is crucial.

MOUNTAIN WILDLIFE

Mountains are home to different animals, depending on where they are in the world. In North America, animals such as bears, moose, wild cats, and mountain sheep are common. Some, such as bears and marmots, **hibernate** during the winter to save energy. During the warmer months, they fatten up for their long sleep. Many animals have developed thick fur to protect them from the cold. Animals that live very high up, such as yaks in the Himalayas, have large hearts and lungs. These bigger organs allow them to live with thinner air and, therefore, less **oxygen** at this height.

A yak in the Himalayan Mountain Range

LOOK OUT!

Look for the "How to Survive" and "Be Prepared" features in this book. These list many of the survival techniques that people have used to survive in the mountains.

Before setting out on a mountain adventure, it is important to take the time to make plans. Explorers should never go into the mountains alone. It is vital to tell others the route and, if possible, to leave a map of the area with them. Essential items to take on a hike or climb include water and climbing equipment. Having emergency equipment can make the difference between survival and death.

PLANNING THE TRIP

In mountainous regions, hikers must check the weather and remember that it can quickly change. Even in warmer weather, it will be cooler higher up the mountain, but the Sun will be stronger and there may be no shade. It is often windier, too. Wearing a hat, sunscreen, lip balm, and layers of clothing help. It is a good idea to take a waterproof jacket too. It is important for explorers to make sure that there is enough time for the hike. Hiking uphill is hard work, and even very fit people cannot do it quickly.

CLIMBING

Alpine climbing is very challenging. It can be very dangerous, especially for people who do not know what they are doing. Climbers have to know how to climb on rock, snow, and ice and be highly skilled in mountain survival. Traditional, or trad, climbing in the wild takes a lot of practice and skill. Even experienced climbers go with a group and many also use a guide who knows the area well. Climbers must use gear, such as **harnesses** and ropes, correctly and safely.

climbing harness

BE PREPARED

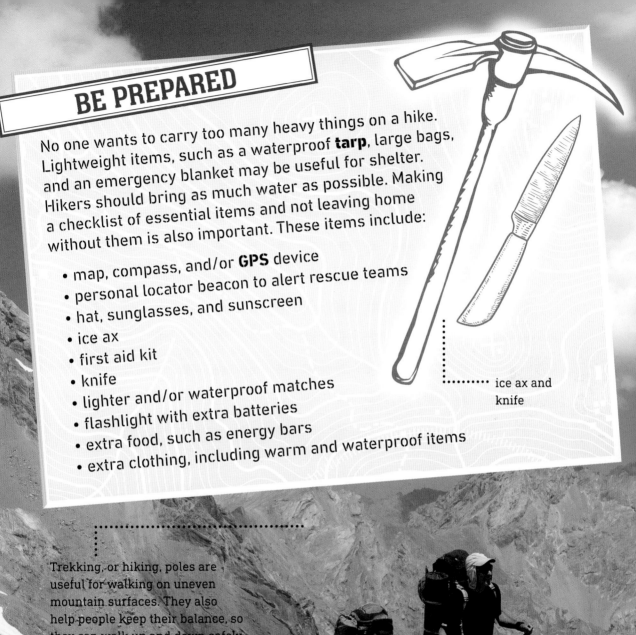

No one wants to carry too many heavy things on a hike. Lightweight items, such as a waterproof **tarp**, large bags, and an emergency blanket may be useful for shelter. Hikers should bring as much water as possible. Making a checklist of essential items and not leaving home without them is also important. These items include:

- map, compass, and/or **GPS** device
- personal locator beacon to alert rescue teams
- hat, sunglasses, and sunscreen
- ice ax
- first aid kit
- knife
- lighter and/or waterproof matches
- flashlight with extra batteries
- extra food, such as energy bars
- extra clothing, including warm and waterproof items

ice ax and knife

Trekking, or hiking, poles are useful for walking on uneven mountain surfaces. They also help people keep their balance, so they can walk up and down safely.

INJURED AND COLD:
GEORGE BROWN

The Rocky Mountains run through Montana in the western United States. George Brown was on an eight-day horseback riding trip in a Montana wilderness park. He was part of a group with a guide. The group made camp one sunny morning, so George thought it would be the perfect time to go for a run. He looked at a trail on a map and showed a friend where he was going. Then, he packed a light lunch, some water, and a flashlight, and he was on his way.

LOSING THE TRAIL

It was sunny when George left the camp, but the skies soon darkened. Blackened logs and **debris** from a forest fire covered the route, so as he kept running, he found it difficult to see the trail. When rain came, George found shelter by a fallen log. After the rain stopped, he realized he could no longer see the trail. George thought he could find his way back to camp by going down the hill to another trail below.

SNAP!

George started to run down the hill, but he slipped and went crashing into a tree. He fell backward and his shin snapped just above his ankle. Moving it was so painful that George just sat for a while. He did not have a first aid kit with him or a phone to call for help. He tried shouting, but there was no answer. He realized that he had no choice but to wait for someone to come and rescue him.

George was 6,000 feet (1,829 m) up in the mountains, and the nighttime was very cold. He wore only a T-shirt and shorts, so he was worried about **hypothermia**. He tried to keep warm by breathing into his

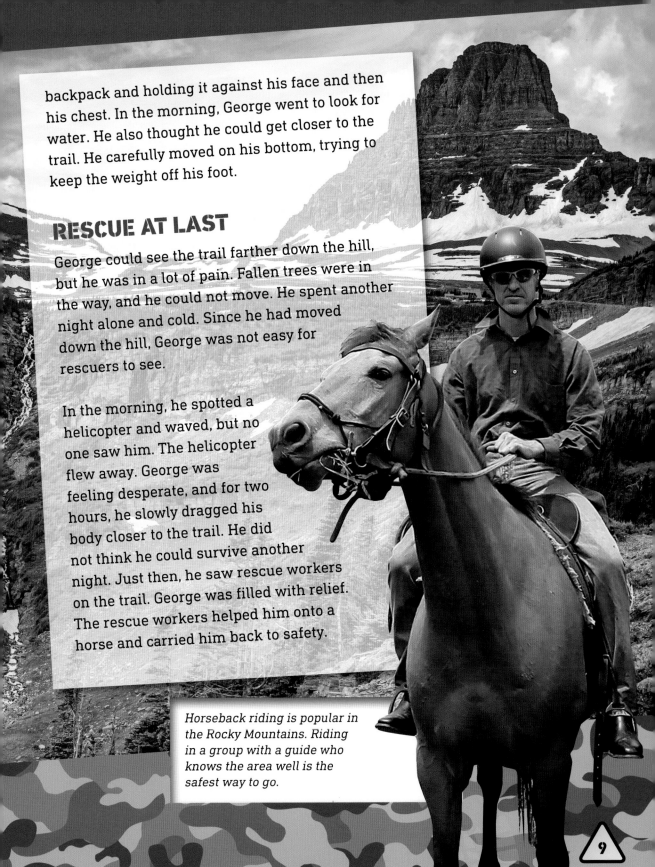

backpack and holding it against his face and then his chest. In the morning, George went to look for water. He also thought he could get closer to the trail. He carefully moved on his bottom, trying to keep the weight off his foot.

RESCUE AT LAST

George could see the trail farther down the hill, but he was in a lot of pain. Fallen trees were in the way, and he could not move. He spent another night alone and cold. Since he had moved down the hill, George was not easy for rescuers to see.

In the morning, he spotted a helicopter and waved, but no one saw him. The helicopter flew away. George was feeling desperate, and for two hours, he slowly dragged his body closer to the trail. He did not think he could survive another night. Just then, he saw rescue workers on the trail. George was filled with relief. The rescue workers helped him onto a horse and carried him back to safety.

Horseback riding is popular in the Rocky Mountains. Riding in a group with a guide who knows the area well is the safest way to go.

Mountain hiking involves walking on uneven surfaces. Mountain trails can be rocky, muddy, or snowy. There may be some steep **inclines** to climb or slopes to walk down. Everyday boots, running shoes, or sandals will not protect the feet in any of these conditions because they do not offer enough support or grip. Hikers must choose the best footwear to avoid trips, falls, and injuries.

HIKING BOOTS

Wearing sturdy hiking or backpacking boots is advised because these have more support. Waterproof and breathable boots keep feet dry. Special hiking socks dry quickly. This is important because wet feet can lead to painful blisters. For traveling higher up where there will be snow, boots should also have **insulation** for warmth.

To prevent blisters, new boots should be worn a few times before a trip.

BE PREPARED

Gaiters keep snow, water, and other debris from getting into boots. They cover the tops of boots or climbing shoes and come in different lengths. They are made from waterproof material. Knee gaiters are useful for deep snow. Mountaineering gaiters are heavier and offer more protection. Some mountaineering boots come with built-in gaiters.

boots with gaiters

CLIMBING SHOES AND BOOTS

Climbers wear different types of shoes, depending on the type of climbing they are doing. Rock climbing shoes are light and flexible. These are good for dry, warmer-weather climbing. Alpine climbers wear boots that let them tackle rock and ice. Before starting on the climbing part of their trip, they wear approach shoes, which are lighter. Higher in the mountains, double boots keep climbers warm. These boots have an inner liner that can be taken out. Climbers put the liners inside their sleeping bags to dry them out quickly or to warm them up.

ANIMAL ADAPTATIONS

Mountain animals have **adapted** to moving around on craggy slopes and snowy **terrain**. Mountain goats' hooves are hard on the outside, so they can push them into ridges in the rock. They have two toes that spread wide for balance. Snow leopards have extra-large feet that are covered in fur. They are like built-in snowshoes for moving on snowy slopes. Their feet are padded to add protection from sharp rocks.

Crampons can be added to most mountaineering boots. They have spikes to allow people to walk over snow and ice.

11

Shelter is very important. Shelters keep people warm when it is cold and provide shade from the hot Sun. They also protect from weather conditions such as rain, wind, and snow. If stranded without a tent, making a shelter may be the only option.

BUILDING MATERIALS

It is important to plan ahead and start building a shelter long before it gets dark. It will take time to find a suitable area in which to make a shelter and also to gather materials. Branches and leaves make a good bed and covering for a shelter. A shelter should be large enough to fit inside, but no larger, so that the body heat from the people inside it warm the shelter.

shelter ·······

IN THE SNOW

If there is a lot of snow and no trees, a small snow trench can be dug or a snow cave can be built for shelter. Although snow shelters are not warm, they help people survive by keeping out the wind and the colder outside temperatures. Inside the snow cave, or any shelter, it is important to stay off the ground. Lying directly on the cold ground causes the body to lose heat. Objects such as tree boughs, leaves, or grasses can be used to make a bed that will be comfortable and insulate against the cold.

CHOOSE A SPOT

Picking a dry spot for a shelter is very important because being wet or damp will cool the body. If possible, a place near a trail is best. This will make it easier for rescuers to find people. However, a shelter should not be built directly on the trail or too close to it, because animals sometimes use trails at night. Large trees with loose branches or areas where an **avalanche** or rockslide may happen must also be avoided.

A shovel makes it much easier to dig a snow cave. Survival shovels fold up so they are easy to carry.

HOW TO BUILD A BRUSH SHELTER

A brush shelter is made from branches from small shrubs or trees and other plant materials. It should include a large branch that is about 4 feet (1.2 m) longer than the body, several other branches, and foliage, or leaves from plants. Any smaller branches are removed from the large branch and it is placed at an angle against a tree. The large branch can be tied with rope to make it more secure. A frame is then created with the other branches and covered with bark and foliage.

Small branches are placed at an angle against a tree.

TRAPPED ON A LEDGE:
DAVID CICOTELLO

David Cicotello and his elder brother Louis loved going on climbing trips together. Both were experienced, but Louis was an expert climber. They looked forward to the challenges in No Man's Canyon, Utah. David and Louis planned their trip for a week in March 2011. Before leaving, David gave a map of their route to his girlfriend, Rhonda. He said he would call her on Thursday, but Rhonda never got the call.

TRAGIC FALL

On the Sunday morning of the trip, David and Louis decided to go on a hike. They planned to **rappel** down the **slot canyon**. The first rappel was 40 feet (12 m), and the second was 100 feet (30.5 m). They had a 200-foot (61 m) rope with them. For the second stage, Louis attached the rope to the anchor and began the descent, or drop. David watched until he could not see Louis but then heard him say that the rope was uneven. Seconds later, the rope ripped through the anchor and disappeared. David shouted for Louis, but there was no response.

NO WAY OUT

David knew that his brother could not have survived the fall. He was filled with grief but also knew that he had to find a way out. David had a rope in his backpack, but it was too short to allow him to climb back up to the place he and Louis had started. For two hours, he tried to find crevices in the rocks for his hands and feet, but he kept slipping. He was trapped in the rocky canyon. In his backpack, David had a little food, some tea, and water. He also had a flashlight, a knife, some socks, a jacket, and some matches.

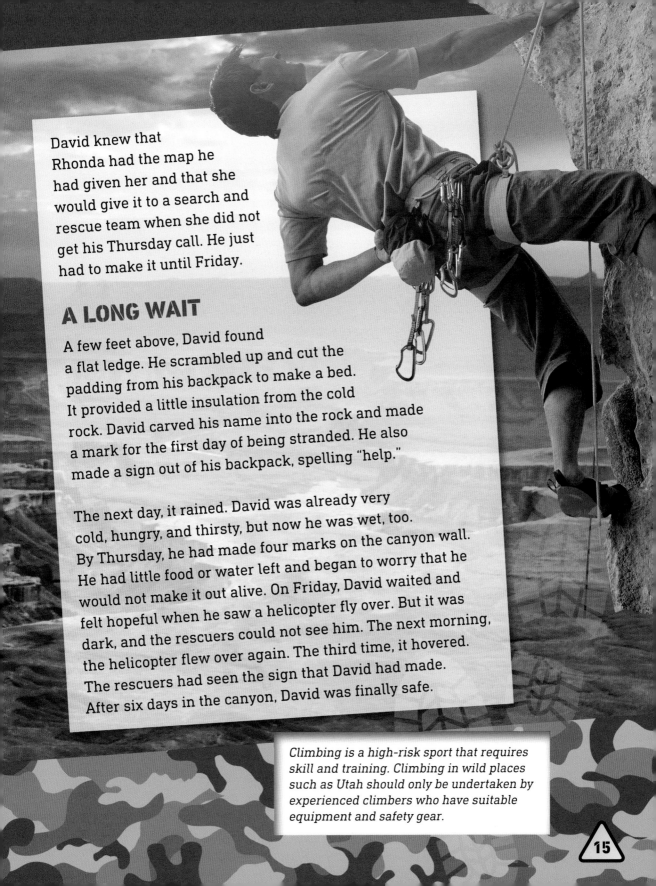

David knew that Rhonda had the map he had given her and that she would give it to a search and rescue team when she did not get his Thursday call. He just had to make it until Friday.

A LONG WAIT

A few feet above, David found a flat ledge. He scrambled up and cut the padding from his backpack to make a bed. It provided a little insulation from the cold rock. David carved his name into the rock and made a mark for the first day of being stranded. He also made a sign out of his backpack, spelling "help."

The next day, it rained. David was already very cold, hungry, and thirsty, but now he was wet, too. By Thursday, he had made four marks on the canyon wall. He had little food or water left and began to worry that he would not make it out alive. On Friday, David waited and felt hopeful when he saw a helicopter fly over. But it was dark, and the rescuers could not see him. The next morning, the helicopter flew over again. The third time, it hovered. The rescuers had seen the sign that David had made. After six days in the canyon, David was finally safe.

Climbing is a high-risk sport that requires skill and training. Climbing in wild places such as Utah should only be undertaken by experienced climbers who have suitable equipment and safety gear.

In most cases, people can only survive three days without water. Mountaineers should bring enough for their trip, but they may run out if they are lost or stranded for a long time. Knowing how to find water and make it safe to drink are lifesaving skills.

HOW MUCH IS ENOUGH?

To stay healthy, people need to drink between 9 to 12.5 cups (2 to 3 liters) of water a day. When it is hot or when they exercise, they need more water so they do not become dehydrated. This happens when the body loses too much water, and it can take just six hours. People also need more water when it is cold and windy because the dry air causes the body to lose water.

BE PREPARED

Even clean-looking water can contain **microbes**, which are tiny life-forms that can make people sick. A mountain survival kit should include water-**purifying** tablets, a plastic bag, and a container for water. Purifying tablets take about 30 minutes to work. Boiling water is the easiest way to purify it. Boiling water for about 10 minutes will kill these "bugs" and make it safe to drink. It is best to strain water through fabric to help remove dirt particles.

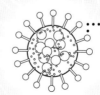

·········· microbe

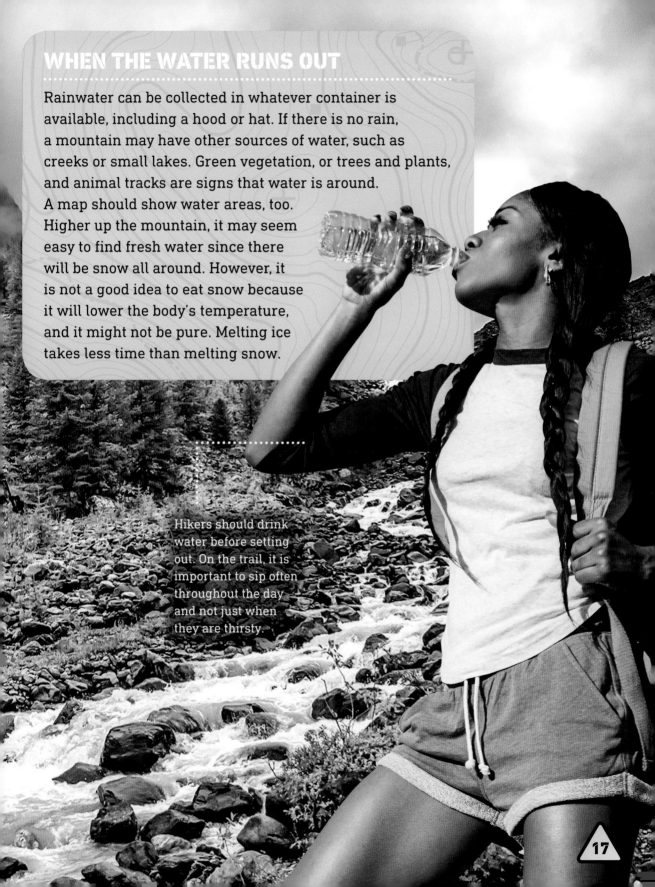

WHEN THE WATER RUNS OUT

Rainwater can be collected in whatever container is available, including a hood or hat. If there is no rain, a mountain may have other sources of water, such as creeks or small lakes. Green vegetation, or trees and plants, and animal tracks are signs that water is around. A map should show water areas, too. Higher up the mountain, it may seem easy to find fresh water since there will be snow all around. However, it is not a good idea to eat snow because it will lower the body's temperature, and it might not be pure. Melting ice takes less time than melting snow.

Hikers should drink water before setting out. On the trail, it is important to sip often throughout the day and not just when they are thirsty.

In snowy mountains, an avalanche is the most feared danger. An avalanche is a massive pile of snow that can travel down a mountain at more than 200 miles per hour (322 km/h). The largest avalanche recorded was 3,000 feet (914 meters) wide. In the case of a slab avalanche, the snow breaks away as a block and moves down the mountain as a powerful wall.

HOW IT HAPPENS

Most avalanches happen during or after a heavy snowfall. Often, the snow is disturbed when it melts or if wind moves it. People may also disturb the snow when they ski or use a snowmobile. Avalanches happen quickly. The upper layer of snow breaks away and moves down the mountain, gathering speed and more snow as it goes.

Skiers should watch and listen for warning signs of an avalanche. A cracking or hollow sound may mean that the skier is traveling near weak layers of snow that may break and move easily.

CAUGHT IN THE SNOW

It is a good rule to avoid skiing, boarding, or snowmobiling alone or in the **backcountry**, unless accompanied by an experienced guide. It is not possible to outrun an avalanche, but it is possible to survive one with training and the right safety equipment. If the avalanche has just started, it is important to stay calm. There may be a chance to move to the side and out of its path. Shouting loudly to others on the mountain will alert everyone so that they, too, can keep watch and move to safety. Gear, such as skis or snowboards, that can pull people into the snow must be dropped and left behind. Emergency airbags are vital equipment. Without an airbag, anyone caught in an avalanche can try to "swim" to keep on top of the snow. If they are buried by the snow, they will need to raise an arm out of the snow so it can be seen.

BE PREPARED

An avalanche survival kit can save lives. It includes a beacon that sends out a signal so rescuers can find people. A small shovel helps to dig a larger air pocket or dig out someone buried in the snow. A probe helps find people under the snow. An airbag brings the body to the surface of the avalanche while it is happening.

avalanche airbag

CAUGHT IN A BLIZZARD:
MATT SMITH AND TOMMY HENDRICKS

Fourteeners are mountains that are more than 14,000 feet (4,267 m) high. Colorado has more than 50 of these mountains. Matt Smith and his friend Tommy Hendricks had hiked and climbed quite a few of them, so they decided to cross the Mount of the Holy Cross off their list.

NOT IN THE PLAN

Tommy started rock climbing with his father when he was around 11 years old. He joined the climbing team in high school and met his best friend, Matt. The two boys were passionate about mountain climbing.

In November 2016, they looked at the weather forecast. It was supposed to be a cold but clear weekend, with a possible storm on Tuesday. Matt and Tommy set out on Sunday and made a camp almost 4 miles (6.4 km) from the beginning of the trail. From there, they thought that it would take about two hours to climb up the steep side of the mountain. But as they climbed higher, the snow was deeper and slowed them down. Then, it began to snow. Matt and Tommy finally reached the top at 7 p.m. Happy they had made it to the top, the friends called their parents and told them that they were safe and would hike down right away.

NO WAY DOWN

By then it was completely dark, and a blizzard, a severe snowstorm, developed. The fierce wind whipped around them, and it was impossible to see a place to go down safely. Tommy and Matt had no choice but to spend the night near the top of the mountain. They found a jagged piece of rock for shelter and tried to keep warm by massaging each other's feet.

Their feet were turning numb and white, which are the first signs of **frostbite**. They stuck their feet in each other's armpits, trying to warm them up. Overnight, it was colder still, and Tommy started worrying about hypothermia.

FINDING A WAY

The next morning was sunny, but the fresh snow made it difficult to find a way down the mountain. Matt and Tommy spotted a creek below and thought they knew where they were going. They rappelled to the creek but realized they were wrong. They were on the other side of the mountain, and now they had no cell phone service. The boys kept moving to keep warm, hoping to find a trail down. As night fell, they tried to build a fire, but their lighters were wet. Huddled together, Matt and Tommy survived another night on the freezing mountainside.

The next day, they forced themselves to get up and hike. A helicopter appeared, so Tommy stuck a red hat on his hiking pole and waved it. The boys stared as the helicopter turned around and flew away. Luckily, it turned out that the helicopter just needed to refuel. It returned an hour later, and the rescuers lifted the boys off the snowy mountain. Tommy and Matt both had frostbite, hypothermia, and were extremely weak, but they had survived their mountain ordeal.

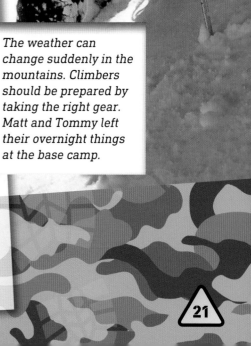

The weather can change suddenly in the mountains. Climbers should be prepared by taking the right gear. Matt and Tommy left their overnight things at the base camp.

Knowing how to navigate, or find the way, is a very important survival skill. The ability to navigate helps people go in the right direction and find their way if they get lost on a mountain. Explorers who travel to the mountains should pack navigation tools, such as maps and compasses, for the journey.

MOUNTAIN MAP WORK

Many people bring modern GPS devices to help find their way. GPS devices are very useful, but their batteries may run out, leaving people stranded. Using an up-to-date map is an essential mountain survival skill. Before the trip begins, the map must be studied to learn about the terrain and learn the route. The map will include a legend, which explains what lines and markings on the map mean.

Checking the map often during the day will help explorers to know exactly where they are. At the same time, explorers should look around and identify features on the map.

FINDING FEATURES

By studying a map, mountaineers find features such as rivers, waterfalls, and hiking trails, as well as possible dangers, such as **crevasses**. During the trip, they should make note of the features as they see them and keep track of the time it takes to travel between locations. Mountain maps will also have contour lines. These are the black, wavy lines on the map that represent **elevations**. The closer together the lines, the steeper the slope. The summit, or top, of the mountain is within a contour ring.

HOW TO USE A COMPASS

A compass shows north, south, east, and west directions. The red needle always points to **magnetic north**, not true north, or the North Pole. The angle between these points is called declination. Maps include the declination, so the compass should be adjusted before leaving. To use the compass, the bezel, or rotating ring, is turned to the direction needed, such as south, so that direction is on top. Then, the compass is held in front of the body, and holding it still, the person turns with it until the red needle is in the red box. When that happens, the person will be facing in the right direction.

compass

Most wild animals will not attack humans unless they have young to protect and feel threatened by people. Humans should keep away from wild animals as much as possible and avoid attracting them by keeping food in metal, animal-proof containers or tied high up in a tree.

LOOKING FOR SIGNS

It is vital to do some research before going to the mountains. This includes finding out which animals live in the area and learning about their habits. One of the surest signs that an animal is in the area is scat, or animal waste. A bear will leave a large amount in one plop, while a bighorn sheep will leave pellets. Scratches or marks on the ground and trees will also give clues. Animals leave these marks when they are looking for food. Some animals, such as mountain lions, are **predators**. Mountain lions may kill an animal and return to feed on it, so its kill must be avoided.

Animals are all around. Singing, yelling, and making noises along the trail will warn animals to stay away.

Many animals migrate, or move from one place to another. In the winter, some animals move down the mountains to warmer areas.

HOW TO RECOGNIZE ANIMAL TRACKS

It is possible to see which animals are in an area by looking at their tracks. Tracks are best seen early in the morning and in the late afternoon, when the Sun is not directly overhead. This is because a low Sun casts shadows in the track, making it easier to see. The size of the prints, whether they show a paw or a hoof, or if there are claw marks are clues to what the animal is. Knowing the differences between different kinds of bears can be helpful. A grizzly bear paw is larger than a black bear paw. Their toe marks will be in a straight line rather than a curve.

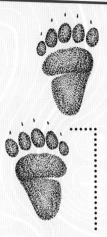

bear tracks

ANIMAL ENCOUNTER

grizzly bear ······

Most animals avoid people, but they can get curious, or they may be attracted by people's food. Bears, for example, will eat most things and could be attracted by the smell of garbage or food that is left out. If an animal approaches, staying calm is important. In most cases, it is not wise to run away since the animal's **instinct** may be to chase. If an animal does start to approach, making a lot of noise by yelling and clapping hands may scare it off. Screaming can sound like a wounded animal, so it is not the right kind of noise to make. It is better to use noisemakers or to bang metal objects together. Mountaineers should make themselves seem as large as possible, or press together if they're in a group, to deter an animal attack.

FLASH FLOOD:
CHRISTINA FIALHO AND J. P. ROSE

It all happened within seconds. Christina Fialho and her boyfriend, J. P. Rose, were enjoying their stop at a beautiful waterfall in the mountains. Christina was resting beside a river underneath the falls. J. P. was in the river, taking photographs. Then, suddenly, a massive surge of muddy water crashed over the waterfall.

A BAD DECISION

Christina and J. P. were on vacation in Guadalupe, a group of islands in the Caribbean. They were staying near Guadalupe National Park, an area of forests and mountains. One afternoon, they decided to go for a hike. When they reached the beginning of the trail, it started to rain. The rain was heavy, but it soon stopped. J. P. and Christina decided to keep going on the muddy trail. It turned out to be the wrong decision.

The couple were at the waterfall for less than an hour when disaster struck. As the powerful gush of water tumbled over the falls, it ripped plants and parts of trees from the earth. Everything hurtled down toward them. Frantically, they climbed up the rocks as the water flooded the area below.

STRANDED

They kept climbing to get away from the water. When they thought they were far enough away, they stopped. Then, they realized that they were stranded. The road was on the other side of the river, and there was no other way back. It began to get dark and rain heavily. J. P. tried his phone, but there was no signal, so they moved to higher ground. He tried again and managed a quick call before he lost the signal.

NOT PREPARED

Christina and J. P. were experienced hikers, but they did not prepare for this particular trip. They had even experienced a **flash flood** before, but they did not think about that when they were enjoying the sunshine by the waterfall. The couple should have taken more notice of the weather and been more aware of any rumbling sounds. Flash floods can happen very quickly, even when the Sun is out.

The pair had not even told anyone where they were going, and they had not packed well. They did not have extra clothes, rain gear, a flashlight, or even a first aid kit. When they found themselves stranded in the wild, they had to wait in their wet clothes. They were cold and wet. It was dark, but Christina found a hollow tree for shelter. They huddled together to try and keep warm. By that time, mosquitoes had come out, and the couple had no protection from their bites.

After almost five hours of being stranded, J. P. and Christina saw lights through the treetops. Luckily, J. P.'s phone had enough power to operate the light. He pointed it upward. It led the rescue helicopter to the couple, and they were finally rescued and taken to safety.

Wearing a t-shirt and shorts is usually fine for a short hike. But, as Christina and J. P. discovered, it is best to pack extra clothes and supplies, just in case disaster strikes.

SURVIVE THE WILD

Mountain regions are challenging places. They can be far from people, and it is easy to get lost there. The weather is changeable, so a sunny day can turn stormy quite quickly. It is also cold up high, even in the summer. People who live in the mountains have adjusted to these challenges. Animals have adapted, too. Visitors must prepare themselves by learning what to expect. They also have to know how to deal with the unexpected.

STAY AND WAIT

Getting lost is always a possibility in the mountains, especially without a map or compass. When lost, it can be tempting to keep looking for a way out, but unless there is danger, such as a rockslide, it is better to stay in the same place. If people have to move, leaving behind a sign will direct rescuers to their new location. Knowing survival skills is vital in the wild—it means staying alive while waiting for rescue.

MAKE A PLAN

When it starts to get dark, it is time to put on extra clothes and find or make a shelter. If it is not raining, there may be dry materials, such as grasses and bark, to make a fire. In the morning, it is time to think about the next steps. This might include finding water and trying to attract rescuers. Rescuers often use helicopters to hover over mountainous areas. Bright-colored clothes will stand out. Rescuers on foot or horseback may hear a whistle. At night, a flashlight may attract attention. In North America, the mountain rescue signal is a light or sound signal made three times. This is followed by a pause of about a minute and then another three signals, and so on.

BE PREPARED

Even on a hike, people may have to climb in some areas. Knowing how to do this safely is important, and it is a good idea to find a climbing wall gym or an outdoor wall to get some training and sharpen skills. Wall climbing is very different from climbing on real rock, however. Trad climbing takes years to learn, so it is always better to start out climbing with easier, lower climbs.

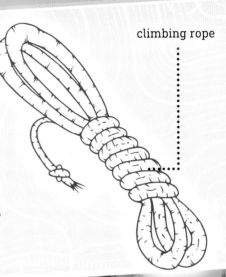

climbing rope

Search and rescue workers take stranded people on board and can perform emergency first aid.

EAT AND DRINK

Emergency rations of high-calorie foods are easy to carry and give energy boosts when stranded. These foods can include protein bars, dried fruit, and energy bars. Taking sips of melted snow throughout the day will help a person stay hydrated.

GLOSSARY

adapted Developed skills or physical features over time to live in a certain biome

alpine Describes something that exists in the high mountains

avalanche The violent and fast-moving movement of a mass of snow down a mountainside

backcountry A wilderness area where few or no people live

biome A large area where plants and animals naturally live. A biome is also recognized by other features, such as how much water it has.

crevasses Deep cracks in ice

debris Scattered pieces of something

elevations Heights

flash flood A sudden, powerful flood, usually after heavy rain

frostbite A condition caused by extreme cold when the muscles and tissues become frozen

glaciers Large areas of ice that move slowly down the side of a mountain

GPS Acronym for Global Positioning System, a system that uses space satellites to help people find their way

harnesses Equipment with straps and belts that is used to keep a person in place while mountain or rock climbing

hibernate To go into a sleep in the winter where the body slows down and feeds on its own fat

hypothermia When a person's body temperature becomes too low, causing serious damage

inclines Slopes

instinct A way of behaving or acting that occurs without learning

insulation Something that protects against the cold

magnetic north The direction a compass needle points when it aligns with Earth's magnetic field

microbes Tiny life-forms that can make a person sick. Viruses, bacteria, and parasites are all microbes.

oxygen A gas in Earth's atmosphere that people and animals need to breathe

predators Animals that hunt and eat other animals

purifying Describes something that can remove harmful substances

range A series of mountains

rappel A way to go down a rock face using a rope fixed at a higher point

slot canyon A long, narrow, and deep channel

tarp A large waterproof piece of cloth or plastic that is rainproof and used as a covering

terrain The land and how it looks

tundra Frozen land with no trees

LEARNING MORE

Find out more about mountains and how to survive them.

Goldish, Meish. *Lost on a Mountain* (Stranded!: Testing the Limits of
   Survival). Bearport, 2014.

Howell, Izzi. *Mountain Geo Facts* (Geo Facts). Crabtree Publishing, 2018.

Spilsbury, Louise. *Surviving the Mountain* (Sole Survivor).
   Gareth Stevens, 2017.

Weber, M. *Surviving the Mountain* (Iron Will). Full Tilt, 2018.

WEBSITES

Check out information about mountain climbing at:
https://kids.britannica.com/kids/article/mountain-climbing/623640

Discover more about the mountain biome at:
**https://kids.nationalgeographic.com/explore/nature/habitats/
mountain**

Find out about surviving North America's highest mountain at:
https://pbskids.org/nova/denali/index.html

Read about other survival stories at:
www.backpacker.com/survival/survival-stories

INDEX

ABOUT THE AUTHOR

Cynthia O'Brien has written many books about exploring the world and the animals that live in its different biomes. She has visited mountains, oceans, and forests. This travel guide and its many useful survival tips will be in her backpack when she travels to the mountains again.